5/01
6X

DATE

PIONEERS IN HEALTH AND MEDICINE

The Life of
Dorothea Dix

PIONEERS IN HEALTH AND MEDICINE

The Life of
Dorothea Dix

Elizabeth Schleichert
Illustrated by Antonio Castro

Twenty-First Century Books

A Division of Henry Holt and Co., Inc.

Frederick, Maryland

Published by
Twenty-First Century Books
A Division of Henry Holt and Co., Inc.
38 South Market Street
Frederick, Maryland 21701

Text Copyright © 1992
Twenty-First Century Books
A Division of Henry Holt and Co., Inc.

Illustrations Copyright © 1992
Twenty-First Century Books
A Division of Henry Holt and Co., Inc.

Printed in Mexico

10 9 8 7 6 5 4 3 2 1

Library of Congress Cataloging in Publication Data
Schleichert, Elizabeth
The Life of Dorothea Dix
Illustrated by Antonio Castro
(A Pioneers in Health and Medicine Book)
Includes index and bibliographical references.
Summary: A biography of the nineteenth-century reformer
who devoted much of her life to improving the treatment of
the mentally ill in the United States.
1. Dix, Dorothea Lynde, 1802-1887—Juvenile literature.
2. Social reformers—United States—Biography—Juvenile
literature. 3. Mentally ill—Care—United States—History—
Juvenile literature. [1. Dix, Dorothea Lynde, 1802-1887.
2. Reformers. 3. Mentally ill—Care—History.]
I. Castro, Antonio, 1941— ill. II. Title. III. Series: Pioneers in
Health and Medicine.
HV28.D6S36 1991 361.92—dc20 [B] 91-29852 CIP AC
ISBN 0-941477-68-1

Contents

1

"If I Am Cold . . ."

Dorothea Dix stepped down carefully from the carriage. A blast of cold wind caused her to clutch her Bible and hymn book closer to her coat. Once inside the jail, Dix was led to a cell where 20 female inmates awaited her. She proceeded with her lesson, leading the women in a Bible reading, a prayer, and a hymn.

Then, she began asking these women questions about themselves. Some, she learned, were criminals who had been in jail for many years. Others had been thrown into prison for public drunkenness. Some had been arrested for stealing. A few women simply had nowhere else to go.

After her lesson, Dix asked the jailer for a tour of the prison. He objected, saying that this was no place for a woman to walk around. But Dorothea Dix was not an easy person to dismiss, and the jailer at last relented. As she followed her reluctant guide down a dimly lit corridor, Dix was horrified at the sight that greeted her. In this section of the prison, the women were chained to the walls of a cold and damp cell. Their clothes were thin, tattered rags. They shivered as the bitter March winds rattled the prison windows.

As she peered into their cell, the stench nearly overwhelmed Dix. She asked who these women were and why they were living in such horrible conditions. The jailer explained to her, in a matter-of-fact manner, that these women were insane.

Suddenly, Dix heard a woman scream—it was a sound she would never forget. At once, she sought out the source of those wretched cries.

Dix found an old woman penned up in a small cage, wailing and cursing. In the same cell, next to the old woman, was a second cage. A younger woman sat in this pen, listening to the screams of her cell-mate. The younger woman's mind was clouded by mental illness, too.

None of the cells in this part of the jail had any furniture. There were no beds or mattresses, not even a bucket for a toilet—just dirty straw strewn around the floor. There was no stove or fireplace to keep these caged inmates warm.

Dorothea kept asking the jailer why these women were here. They had lost their minds, he explained, and could no longer take care of themselves. So they were being housed out of the public's way. Clearly, the jailer was beginning to lose his patience with this

inquisitive visitor. Didn't everyone know that many "lunatics" were locked up?

"Why don't these poor souls have heat in their cells?" Dix persisted.

"Mad people don't need stoves, ma'am," he said. "They don't feel the cold. And, besides, it would be dangerous. They could start a fire in the jail, burn the whole place down."

The conditions that Dorothea Dix saw at the East Cambridge jail should have brought compassion from the most hardhearted of onlookers. But in 1841, such conditions were common.

At that time, prisons and poorhouses frequently took in mentally ill people, usually those who had no money and no family to care for them. The women Dix saw had committed no crime. Their only offense was to be sick and to have no place else to go.

But these innocent prisoners were often abused. They were kept in cold, unheated cells, or locked in tiny pens; they were chained and whipped; they were poorly fed and clothed, or simply left in filthy rooms, where they were exposed to a variety of diseases.

For thousands of years, mentally ill people had been objects of hatred, fear, and cruelty. Since ancient times, mental illness was considered a sign that evil spirits or demons possessed the body. It was seen as a punishment from the gods or as a kind of witchcraft. The "treatment" most often given the mentally ill was torture, persecution, and even death.

Throughout history, there had always been a few people who rejected the idea that mental illness was the work of evil spirits or the gods. The ancient Greek physician Hippocrates claimed that mental disorders resulted from natural causes. At the end of the Middle Ages, the German doctor Paracelsus said that "mental diseases have nothing to do with spirits or devils." But such ideas were rarely voiced, and rarely heard.

As Dorothea Dix was to learn through decades of observation, the treatment of the mentally ill had not improved very much over the years. Almost without exception, what passed for treatment was shamefully abusive. In most cases, there was really no treatment at all.

The mentally ill were usually locked away, sent to places where they could be kept out of sight. If they could not afford a private hospital, they were sent to local poorhouses or prisons, where they faced cruel conditions. Sometimes, they were even auctioned off as laborers—simply sold to the highest bidder.

Dorothea Dix refused to allow these conditions to remain hidden. Her work brought attention to a situation that most people preferred to ignore.

"It is truly sorrowful to find so much suffering through ignorance and neglect," she wrote.

Her cause was the welfare of a group of men and women who, because of sickness, had been cast out from family, from community, from society—a group of people who were not treated as human beings.

Dix's accomplishments were many, but none was more important than the fact that she brought hope to the medically outcast.

"If I am cold," she wrote, "they, too, are cold. If I am weary, they are distressed. If I am alone, they are abandoned."

When Dorothea Dix left the Cambridge jail, she walked into the bright sunlight. She saw clearly what she had to do.

2

Leaving Home

Dorothea Dix was born on April 4, 1802, in the backwoods of northern Massachusetts. Very little is known about her childhood. But what is known of these years suggests a life of poverty and neglect. "I never knew childhood," Dix wrote years later.

In 1802, the village of Hampden, Massachusetts (now a part of Maine), was a frontier settlement of several hundred people. Hampden was not an easy place to get to. Settlers had to travel up the Penobscot River and then hike through the dense forests of the rugged Massachusetts countryside. Those people who did manage to reach the Hampden settlement soon found that the physical hardships of frontier life were even more difficult.

Deep in this New England wilderness, Elijah Dix, Dorothea Dix's grandfather, had bought thousands of acres of undeveloped land. A successful Boston doctor and businessman, Elijah Dix hoped to build new towns in these distant woods. He sent his son Joseph to manage the property for him.

Joseph was the third son of Elijah and Dorothy Dix. Unlike his successful father, Joseph was not an ambitious man. He seemed to drift from one interest to another. Perhaps, Elijah Dix thought, the ruggedness of the New England frontier would give Joseph a sense of discipline and direction.

But Joseph was no more successful at carving a career out of the Massachusetts woods than he had been at finding one in the city of Boston. By the time Dorothea was born, her father, like other settlers, had cleared a small patch of farmland from the frontier. The Dixes lived in a plaster-chinked log house. It was little more than a single room. A central fireplace and oil-paper windows barely kept out the cold.

Coping with this wilderness area was a constant challenge. Survival there required long hours of hard work for both men and women—clearing, planting, and harvesting the fields; making and mending the family's clothes; tending the garden; and preserving fruits and vegetables. For adults, there was little time for rest. For children, there was little time for play.

Each day brought a full round of chores for the children of the wilderness settlement to do: working in the fields, hauling wood and water, sewing clothes, tending the livestock, and caring for younger brothers and sisters.

Neither of Dorothea's parents was able to meet the challenge of the frontier. Mary Dix was often sick or too depressed to work. Joseph turned out to be a poor land manager and a bad farmer. He seems to have been prone to fits of restlessness and instability. It wasn't long before Joseph abandoned his efforts at supervising his father's property and making a home for his family.

Joseph had studied religion at college. Now he decided to become a traveling preacher. He rode off on horseback to preach to the scattered villages of the frontier. Joseph's religion was a rigid and harsh one. His sermons spoke of an angry God and the bitter fate that awaited the many sinners of the world.

Joseph's "calling" to save the people of the New England wilderness resulted in further hardship for his own family. He was gone for long periods of time, and the money he made from his preaching was not enough to support his family.

To earn more money, Joseph sold copies of his sermons. He would return to Hampden with a sheaf of sermons printed on long sheets of paper. The sheets had to be cut, folded, and sewn together. Dorothea spent hours bent over the pamphlets, forcing a needle through thick layers of paper.

Dorothea also had to watch her younger brothers, Joseph and Charles Wesley. Mary Dix never regained her strength after the birth of her second son (about

1808). It was up to Dorothea, at age six, to assume the role of mother to her two little brothers.

Burdened by these responsibilities, Dorothea Dix grew up with little love or support from her parents. One of her relatives described the Hampden home as "miserable and loveless." Dorothea herself said that she was "early taught to shed tears."

Dorothea's only escape from a joyless childhood were her trips to the home of her grandparents. Elijah and Dorothy Dix lived in a beautiful home called Dix Mansion. For a young girl growing up in a log cabin, Dix Mansion was a place filled with treasures.

There were rooms crowded with rich furniture. There were elegant pictures on the walls and brass candlesticks on the tables. There were many curious knickknacks that hinted of worlds beyond Dorothea's imagination—conch shells that caught the enchanting sounds of the sea and wonderfully colored coral from some faraway shore. When Dorothea looked into the brightly polished bowls and plates set for the dinner table, she could see her reflection.

A visit to Boston brought Dorothea freedom from the daily routine of work. She had time to wander in her grandmother's lovely flower garden or spend a quiet moment in the mansion's library.

And she had time to enjoy the company of her grandfather. Elijah Dix returned his granddaughter's need for affection with kindness and attention.

Sometimes, Dorothea would go with her grandfather in his horse-drawn carriage when he went to see his patients. As they bumped along the cobblestone streets, Dorothea was fascinated by the sights and sounds of Boston. Her grandfather's stories about the exciting days of the Boston Tea Party and Paul Revere's famous ride delighted her, too.

On occasion, Dorothea visited her grandfather's apothecary shop, where he prepared medicines from rows of strange brown and blue bottles. Other times, they stopped to catch a view of Boston harbor and the forest of tall-masted ships resting at anchor. If they were fortunate, the two of them would watch a ship setting forth for a distant port, its graceful white topsails billowing in the breeze.

Such visits to Boston never lasted long enough. When Dorothea returned home, she found that things were more and more difficult. Joseph began showing signs of increasing restlessness. On a whim, he would try a different profession for a while, moving his family to a different town—only to move again and return to preaching when his new job didn't work out. The family rarely stayed in one place for long.

At age 12, Dorothea left this "loveless home." She either ran away from home to Dix Mansion, or her family decided to send her there. The facts about the move are vague. In any case, her beloved grandfather had died five years before. Her grandmother was a widow. Madam Dix, now 68 years old, agreed to let Dorothea live with her.

At first, Dorothea was excited to be back. But she soon found out that visiting Boston during her grandfather's lifetime was very different from living there with her strict and demanding grandmother.

Madam Dix loved Dorothea, but she believed in doing her duty more than in open displays of love and affection. Her duty in this case, as she saw it, was to make a lady out of her backwoods granddaughter.

Madam Dix insisted that Dorothea must be neat, punctual, respectful, and obedient. Dorothea was sent to a private school, where she was an eager student, but her grandmother's attempts to mold Dorothea's manners were not very successful. Dorothea rebelled against the demands of Madam Dix. To Dorothea, it seemed that no matter how hard she tried to please her grandmother, Madam Dix managed to find fault with her.

Dorothea hated having to follow so many rules. She felt alone and sorry for herself. First, her parents hadn't loved her, and now, she was convinced, her grandmother disliked her, too.

For her part, Madam Dix didn't have the strength to bring up her independent-minded granddaughter. In 1816, two years after Dorothea moved in with her grandmother, Madam Dix asked her sister, Sarah, to take Dorothea for a while. Sarah lived in Worcester, some 40 miles west of Boston.

So a lonely Dorothea, now 14 years old, was put on a stagecoach to Worcester. As the coach pulled out of Boston, it carried its solitary traveler west over the rutted Boston Post Road. Dorothea Dix was leaving home again.

3

A Pattern of Excellence

Dorothea Dix found a new home—and a happy one—with her relatives in Worcester. Gentle words of praise and encouragement took the place of Madam Dix's impatient commands.

Dorothea was also welcomed into a new circle of friends. Surrounded by companions close to her own age, she went for walks along Worcester's main street. There, they showed her the towering elms that her grandfather, Elijah Dix, once presented to the town as a gift. They invited Dorothea to picnics and rowing parties on Lake Quinsigamond. For the first time in her life, Dorothea felt accepted and loved.

She also enjoyed the companionship of one of her older cousins, Edward Bangs. He was 28, almost twice her age. The handsome and worldly young man had studied law with his father and was just beginning a legal and political career. Edward and Dorothea spent hours discussing art, religion, and literature.

Many people thought that Dorothea and Edward were in love. It was rumored that they were engaged to be married, but the truth is not known. Dorothea never discussed this matter, and no letters between her and Edward have survived. Whatever the case, something happened to end the relationship. It was Dorothea's first—and last—romantic involvement.

While Dorothea was in Worcester, she began the career that was to sustain her for the next 20 years. Though only a teen-ager, she was already driven by a need to be active and to help others. She asked her aunt for permission to open a school.

Aunt Sarah thought the idea was worth a try. The school would be a good place for the younger cousins, and it might provide an outlet for some of Dorothea's unbounded energy. Though she was not much older than some of her pupils, Dorothea made herself look more mature by dressing in somber greys and blacks, lengthening her skirts, and pulling her hair back.

Set up in an old printing shop, Dorothea's school was quite a popular one, with as many as 20 children attending. Dorothea taught such basic skills as reading and writing. She also instructed her students in social skills and customs—the kinds of manners that Dorothea herself had resisted at Dix Mansion. Morals and religion were given special attention, and every child was required to recite a different passage from the Bible each week.

The young teacher was reported to have "a very stern expression." When necessary, Dorothea would whip her students to enforce discipline. One of her students later remarked, "I don't know that she had any special grudge against me, but it was her nature to use the whip, and use it she did." And one little girl who had somehow displeased Dorothea had to walk back and forth to school with a sign on her back that read, "A Very Bad Girl, Indeed."

Dorothea ran the school for nearly three years. But her stay in Worcester came to an end when she received word that her grandmother wanted her to return to Dix Mansion. Now 73 years old, the lonely Madam Dix hoped that her granddaughter might be a loving companion.

Madam Dix must have been pleasantly surprised to see how much Dorothea had changed. Gone was the unruly, willful little girl who had objected to her grandmother's rules and restrictions. At 17, Dorothea was well mannered and mature.

However, Dorothea had not lost her independent spirit or her determination to find meaningful work. Dorothea wanted to be a teacher, but she knew that she needed more education. Madam Dix arranged for Dorothea to continue her schooling. She even hired tutors for private training.

Dorothea could often be found in one of Boston's many public libraries. She enjoyed reading about history and studying literature. She was also intrigued by new discoveries in science and attended lectures on astronomy, geology, and botany.

For Dorothea, Boston was a stimulating place. In the 1820s, new ideas were beginning to replace the rules of New England's religious founders. Religious leaders began to stress the basic goodness of people, rather than their sinful and wicked nature. The beliefs of the religion called Unitarianism, as taught by the preacher William Ellery Channing, revolved around the love of God instead of fear. Channing's emphasis was on personal improvement, not damnation. More and more, Boston was alive with ideas about how to make the world we live in a better place.

Dorothea listened intently to Rev. Channing as he preached these doctrines. The popular minister of the Federal Street Church, Channing was an impressive speaker. His voice took on a fervent and spellbinding cadence as he spoke; his eyes seemed to come alive with confidence. Dorothea was inspired by his message of hope, and Channing soon became a valuable friend and teacher to her.

Here was a religious leader who did not preach, as her father had, about humanity's evil ways. He did not preach about a God who was vengeful and cruel. Rather, Channing spoke of goodness and a merciful, loving God. Those people who showed their essential goodness glorified God, Channing suggested. "Every human being has in him the germ of the greatest idea in the universe, the idea of God," he wrote.

To bring out this inner divinity, to reach religious perfection—this is the purpose of human life, Channing thought. To make ourselves and our world better is the essence of Christian charity, he said, pointing out that "Christ preached to the poor."

These were words of great comfort to Dorothea. This was a faith that she could embrace, a faith that assured her that she was loved.

In the everyday world, Dorothea later wrote, we have "no certain trust, no enduring home." She had learned this unhappy lesson as a child. But now she felt that she had found a home, a home in the love of God. Dorothea had come to believe that a loving God would provide a place of shelter and safety for her. "He will prepare a place for thee," she wrote, "and thou shall not call thyself an orphan."

In religion, Dorothea at last found a direction for her energy. She began a course of self-improvement. A lonely childhood had encouraged in Dorothea the habit of self-examination. Now, she started to study her thoughts, emotions, and actions in a struggle to rise above her own imperfections.

She wrote that "the duty of self-examination is one of the most difficult which we are called to perform." But only by "discipline and hourly trial," she believed, could people reach religious perfection.

This interest in self-improvement was shared by Dorothea's friend, Anne Heath. As a companion and confidante, Anne was always a source of comfort in Dorothea's life.

Both Dorothea and Anne were influenced by Rev. Channing's emphasis on the potential good in people; both were determined to carry through a program of intellectual and moral self-improvement. In hundreds of letters and notes, they recorded the details of their lives—what sermons they had attended, what books they had read. They encouraged one another on the quest for religious perfection and provided support during times of sadness and distress.

But their friendship was not always so serious. Their letters display the kind of affection and intimacy rarely found in Dorothea's life. Dorothea would sign herself "Thea," and Anne often reversed her friend's name, addressing her as "Theodora."

Dorothea especially enjoyed a visit to the Heaths' home, where she was welcomed as a member of the family. "I always leave your house with regret," she wrote to Anne, "and feel that there I might be happy."

Dorothea often compared Anne's family with her own solitary life: "You have an almost angelic mother, Anne; you cannot but be both good and happy while she hovers over you, ministering to your wants, and supplying all that the fondest affection can provide. Your sisters, too, comfort you. I have none."

It was in the classroom that Dorothea felt a sense of connection to people. For Dorothea Dix, teaching was an answer to loneliness, a route to the happiness that she had never found before.

Dorothea said that being a teacher was "elevating and exciting" work. It was much more than a job for her. It was a means of self-improvement; it was a way of helping others. "While surrounded by the young," she wrote, "one may always be doing good."

To her, no feeling compared to that of watching the progress of one of her students:

> *What greater bliss than to look back on days spent in usefulness, in doing good to those around us, in fitting young spirits for their native skies; the duties of a teacher are neither few nor small but they elevate the mind and give energy to the character. They shed light like religion on the darkest hours and like faith they lead us to realms on high.*

In the early 1820s, Dorothea opened a school at Dix Mansion. It took some persuading to get Madam Dix to agree, but by now Dorothea had learned how to be quite persuasive. When this school proved itself a success, Dorothea began a similar program for poor children. Dorothea said that she wanted her "charity school," called The Hope, to "rescue children from vice and guilt."

Dorothea's dedication to her teaching was clear. She mastered many new subjects and authored books for young readers, including an encyclopedia called *Conversations on Common Things*.

Published in 1824, this work covered nearly 300 topics and was designed to answer the kinds of questions that Dorothea regularly heard from her students. How is a book printed? What makes a clock work? How do vegetables grow? One reviewer wrote that the author understood "the importance of giving to American children knowledge as will be actually useful to them, instead of filling their minds with vague, and therefore useless, notions of subjects."

In the introduction to the encyclopedia, Dorothea stated that her "highest ambition" was "the improvement of children, and their advancement in the pathway of learning." She dedicated the encyclopedia to her "young pupils with the wish that it might inform their minds and excite them to seek after knowledge."

Her wish to inform the minds of young people apparently came true. *Conversations on Common Things* was printed a second time, and then a third time; by 1869, it had gone through 60 printings!

Teaching and writing required constant attention. "You know well," Dorothea wrote Anne Heath, "that the measure of my days is filled with constant business—teaching, and learning, reading, and writing." There was "little leisure," she said, "for amusements of any kind." Dorothea rose before dawn and began her day reading the Bible. She often ended her work long after midnight.

But Dorothea's joy in teaching and her success as a writer were overshadowed by her declining health. She developed lung congestion and was ordered to stay in bed. Dorothea's schools had to be shut down while she regained her strength.

It was always hard for Dorothea to "take it easy." Even while she was sick, she continued her writing, working on books of moral tales and religious ideas. These books reflected the confidence and joy she had found in religion.

Her thoughts for the Sabbath stress the idea of self-improvement, of trying to be perfect, as taught by Rev. Channing and other Unitarians:

> *On this day, Sabbath of the Soul, I would especially avail myself of the benefits to be derived from contemplating the life of Jesus Christ. His life presents a pattern of excellence which I can never hope to equal but must daily strive to imitate. I must not be dispirited because I cannot at once be on earth, perfect, but rather animated that I have such aids, "To help me on to heaven."*

In the spring of 1831, Dorothea was well enough to work again. She proceeded to open what was to be her last school. Boston was now establishing schools for girls, and Dorothea was interested in trying her hand at such an institution.

With renewed vigor and her old determination, Dorothea threw herself into her work. Her reputation as a good teacher was well established, and her school attracted girls from other states as boarders, as well as day pupils from the Boston area.

As before, Dorothea Dix stressed that knowledge was a means of self-improvement, a way to develop a strong character and clean conscience. She urged even the youngest of her students to conduct a daily self-examination. This was the only way, she felt, that they could overcome their faults and nurture good traits.

Dorothea Dix had been her own harshest critic for years, striving always to better herself. She wanted her students to do the same. To insure their success, Dorothea asked them to keep her informed, through written notes to her, about their progress.

One such note reveals the sincerity with which her students undertook this assignment:

> *You wished me to be very frank and tell you my feelings. I feel the need of someone to whom I can pour forth my feelings, they have been pent up so long. You may, perhaps, laugh when I tell you I have a disease, not of body but of mind. This is unhappiness. Can you tell me anything to cure it? If you can, I shall indeed be very glad. I am in*

constant fear of my lessons, I am so afraid that I shall miss them. I think that if I do, I shall lose my place in the school, and you will be displeased with me.

For five years, Dorothea continued her work. But in the spring of 1836, at the age of 34, she suffered a physical and emotional breakdown more serious than any illness she had ever battled.

Dorothea Dix was forced to close her school. Her physician, Dr. Hayward, feared that she might never regain her health. Her letters to Anne Heath reflect Dorothea's own fear that a premature end was near. "I feel it is very possible," she wrote, "I may never again enjoy the fragrances of spring."

4

Some Nobler Purpose

Dr. Hayward urged his patient to rest, but that seemed to be a prescription that Dorothea Dix could not accept. From her sickbed, she composed religious hymns and made plans for the future of her school.

It was clear that Dix would never fully recover unless she managed to put aside her teaching duties. So Dr. Hayward advised her to take a trip abroad. Away from daily cares and concerns, he hoped, Dix might find the rest that would restore her health.

Dorothea Dix hoped so, too. Shortly before her trip, she prayed that "rest might be found; and that the most High may bring me out of darkness into the light of health."

On April 22, 1836, Dorothea Dix, frail and sickly, set sail for England. Dorothea's weakened condition was worsened by the voyage, and when she finally arrived in Liverpool, it was apparent that she was too ill to go any further.

Fortunately, Dix brought along a letter of introduction from Rev. Channing to one of his friends in Liverpool, a fellow Unitarian by the name of William Rathbone. Rathbone insisted that Dix come at once to his country home, Greenbank, a peaceful, rural retreat three miles outside of Liverpool. She was given her own room, and she settled in to rest and recuperate.

Writing home, Dix described her visit with the Rathbones. "Imagine me," she wrote, "surrounded by every comfort, sustained by every tenderness that can cheer, blest in the continual kindness of this family." Indeed, Dix was welcomed into the Rathbone home as if she were an old friend. Her stay at Greenbank was "the sunniest, the most restful" period she had known for years. Slowly, her spirits and her body mended.

William Rathbone, a successful businessman, had been involved in trying to right the injustices he saw around him. In the 1800s, England was suffering from serious problems caused by the growth of city-based factories. The country's economy had been disrupted. Masses of poor laborers, whose jobs were lost to the factories, pressed into squalid slums, looking for work of any sort. City after city presented a crowded scene of poverty and disease.

Many concerned people took part in attempts to solve these problems. Outside of Liverpool, a stream of visitors enlivened the Rathbones' home with talk of how to address such problems. Dix had similar concerns about conditions in the towns of New England. Once she recovered some of her strength, she began meeting these guests and joining the talk of reform.

One of the guests at Greenbank was Dr. Samuel Tuke. Through him, Dorothea undoubtedly heard of the work of his father, William Tuke. A visit to the York County Asylum, whose inmates were mentally ill, had shocked and angered the elder Tuke. He saw patients who were chained and penned. He saw men and women, whose only "offense" was mental illness, being treated more like wild animals. In 1792, Tuke founded his own asylum called York Retreat.

The treatment of the mentally ill at York Retreat followed the reforms suggested by Philippe Pinel, a Frenchman whose humane ideas had earned him the title of "liberator of the insane." Pinel had reviewed his country's treatment facilities for the mentally ill. Based on his observations, Pinel presented his own ideas in a book on "the diseases of the mind."

Pinel advocated the removal of chains and other forms of restraint. He also stressed that a healthy diet, plenty of exercise, productive work, and simple kindness and concern were the most likely ways to restore health to the mentally ill. William Tuke adopted these reforms, and York Retreat became a model of humane treatment of the insane.

Dorothea Dix felt a bond of sympathy with the Rathbones and their charitable friends. At Greenbank, she later wrote, "hearts met hearts, minds joined with minds." With each day, Dorothea grew more eager to undertake some sort of socially useful work.

And with each day, she also grew more restless. "Nothing seems so likely to make people unhappy," she said, "than the habit of killing time." She had no idea yet what direction her social service would take. But she admired the work of her English friends, and she awaited a calling of her own:

> *No day, no hour comes but brings in its train work to be performed for some useful end— the suffering to be comforted, the wandering led home, the sinner reclaimed. Oh, how can any fold the hands to rest and say to the spirit, "Take thine ease for all is well."*

Dix's restful days at Greenbank were interrupted by news from home. In September 1836, she learned her mother had died in New Hampshire. (Her father had died in 1821.) The following June, word came that Madam Dix had died after a long illness.

For Dorothea Dix, these losses seemed to leave her more and more alone, cut off from the network of relationships that the people around her enjoyed. She wrote to Anne that Madam Dix's death had "divided the only link which binds me to kindred."

It was not until the fall of 1837 that Dix was well enough to return to the United States. She had spent

18 months at Greenbank, having "drunk deeply, long, and blissfully," she said, of the Rathbones' kindness and affection.

Upon her return, she had to face a world that had changed—her friends had moved away, her old home now belonged to others. It was easy to think about the friends she had made at Greenbank, the people who shared her vision of self-improvement and social usefulness. But Dorothea Dix was only 35 years old. It was the future she should be thinking about. "Life is not to be expended in vain regrets," she wrote.

What was she to do with her life? This was the question that occupied Dix for the next several years. Her health would not permit her to teach. What else was she prepared to do?

She could live on the money Madam Dix had left her and the earnings she received from her published books. But it was not enough just to live, Dix felt. She needed to live for some useful end, some purpose that gave life meaning and value.

She traveled somewhat aimlessly—a "wanderer," she called herself. She wrote that she was depressed by the inactivity of her life: "I longed for some nobler purposes for which to labor, something which would fill the vacuum which I felt in my soul."

"Perhaps it is within myself the fault lies," Dix confessed to Anne. She wondered what was wrong with her that she was unable to find direction.

The world outside was brimming with reformist movements—women's rights, the abolition of slavery, humane treatment for the disabled—and Boston was the hub of new ideas and social change. But for Dix the question remained: "What should I do?"

The answer appeared one day quite by chance. It was March of 1841, and Dorothea Dix was staying at a friend's house. One day, a young man named John Nichols came to visit. He was a student at Harvard Divinity School. Dix was an old friend of his family.

Nichols and some classmates had been assigned to teach Sunday school to women prisoners at the East Cambridge jail. But it soon became clear to them that this was a job more suited to a mature woman than to young male students. Nichols had come to ask Dix if she knew someone who might help.

Nichols later recounted her reply:

> *On hearing my account, Miss Dix said after some deliberation, "I will take them myself." I protested her physical incapacity as she was in feeble health. "I shall be there next Sunday," was her answer.*

The next Sunday, March 28, 1841, Dorothea Dix *was* there. She had come to the East Cambridge jail to teach religion to the women prisoners.

When Dorothea Dix entered the East Cambridge jail on that cold March day in 1841, she had no idea that her life was about to be changed. She went to the prison to teach Sunday school, to pass on the lesson of charity that offered her comfort, the lesson of love that offered her strength.

But the conditions that Dorothea Dix found there soon became, for her, the truest test of those lessons.

Upon leaving the jail, she could not put out of her mind the images she had seen—the picture of hungry and cold women huddled in damp, dirty cells. She could not forget the screams she had heard. She could not forgive the unfeeling replies of the jailer.

Dorothea Dix refused to let the matter rest.

Dix took her concerns to the Cambridge Court. Women were not allowed to speak before the court, but they could state their case in writing. Dorothea Dix described the conditions she had witnessed at the East Cambridge jail—the filthy cells, the lack of heat, the cages unfit for animals. She appealed to the court to provide stoves for the inmates.

Dix's compassion and concern were greeted with anger and disbelief. People were outraged that someone would make such charges about their community. The newspapers mocked her openly.

Still, Dorothea Dix would not be silent. She was determined to make the people of Boston aware of the way they treated their mentally ill neighbors. If they would not listen to her, then she would find others who would support her cause.

Dix wrote letter after letter describing what she had seen at the Cambridge jail. She wanted to inform Boston's community leaders about this matter. If they were made aware of the situation, they would have to take action. Surely, they would be outraged. Late into the night, Dix worked.

Samuel Gridley Howe, who was working to help the disabled children of Boston, soon became an ally. Dorothea Dix urged Howe to see for himself the truth of her account.

In September 1841, an article by Howe appeared in a Boston newspaper. Howe reported in detail the abuses at the jail, confirming what Dorothea Dix had already stated in her court case. Howe's article set off a new wave of objections, and critics also called his report a lie.

At Dix's request, Charles Sumner, a prestigious Boston legislator, had accompanied Samuel Howe on his visit to the Cambridge jail. He supported Samuel Howe's article, writing an account of his visit that was widely published. In one part of Sumner's report, he depicted the scenes that Dorothea Dix had witnessed weeks before.

"I am sorry to say," Sumner later wrote to Dix, "that your article does present a true picture of the conditions in which we found those unfortunates."

With these men reporting such facts, the public could not help but take notice. The court listened, too, and a stove was provided for the mentally ill inmates of the Cambridge jail.

Meanwhile, Dix had begun to question whether this jail was unique. Were the mentally ill neglected elsewhere, she wondered? Dix gathered information by talking with knowledgeable people and reading all she could about the subject herself.

What she discovered distressed her. Across the country, states had been slow to build asylums for the care and treatment of the mentally ill. In fact, in 1841, there were only 14 mental hospitals in the country, enough to care for only a small fraction of those who needed help. As a result, many of the insane were sent to prisons and poorhouses. Others were auctioned off to serve as farm servants.

Even for those mentally ill patients who were put in asylums, there was no scientific treatment. At many asylums, the methods of treatment were often violent and abusive. They included tying patients to straight chairs for hours on end, depriving them of food for long periods of time, or dousing them with ice-cold water. It would be the work of later generations to develop more scientific methods of treatment for the mentally ill.

In the meantime, the poor and homeless mentally ill suffered the most. Wealthy people could pay for special attendants to care for their mentally ill family members. They could afford to send them to one of the country's private hospitals, such as the McLean Psychiatric Hospital, outside Boston.

Dorothea Dix decided to visit McLean and was impressed by what she saw. McLean was similar to what Samuel Tuke had told her about York Retreat. The patients there were treated more humanely than in large asylums. They were allowed to exercise and to pursue activities that interested them. It was unfair, Dix thought, that this kind of care was available only to those who could afford it.

Clearly, there were many abuses in the treatment of the mentally ill. But few attempts had been made to study this subject when Dorothea Dix began to take an interest in it. Dix knew that if more asylums were to be built in Massachusetts, a careful report of the present state of care for the mentally ill would have to be prepared for the state lawmakers.

Someone had to inspect every jail and almshouse across the state where the mentally ill were kept. Only a case-by-case survey of conditions would be effective. The lawmakers would have to be shocked—and shamed—into awareness and action.

Slowly, Dix came to believe that she herself was the person to undertake this task. Friends like Anne Heath tried to talk her out of the idea.

This was no job for a woman, they said. It would ruin her health. She would have to travel more than 8,000 square miles, visiting every tiny hamlet in the state. Transportation was poor—there were only three train lines in the state of Massachusetts. Dix would have to take stagecoaches or private carriages much of the time. A woman traveling by herself was cause for gossip, and, besides, there were unknown dangers on the road. Even such supporters as Samuel Howe and Charles Sumner tried to dissuade Dix from such an ambitious undertaking.

Dorothea Dix turned to her friend and mentor, Rev. Channing, for advice. Now very sick, Channing could sense Dix's excitement at the prospect of doing this good work. He saw how she burned with a new-found certainty of purpose. At last, he thought, she had found a way—her way—to better the world. He held out his hand and gave Dix his blessing.

Dorothea Dix set out on the crusade to which she would dedicate her life. "This was the beginning," she wrote. "I saw the path marked out for me."

5

A Grim Tale

For a year and a half, Dorothea Dix traveled the length and breadth of the state of Massachusetts, from the densely forested western mountains to the sandy Atlantic shore. Every dark corner, every hidden shed, and every cold cell; every poorhouse and jail—there was no place that escaped Dix's notice.

With notebook in hand, Dix recorded what she saw. She soon learned that, in places throughout the state, conditions were far worse than those she had seen at the Cambridge jail.

Day after day, Dix made her journal entries. A grim tale of abuse gradually unfolded.

Dorothea Dix demanded to see the inmates that society preferred to keep out of sight. In one town, she found a man who had been locked in a cage for more than 17 years.

At the poorhouse in Newburyport, a woman was kept beneath the stairs. "As we descended the stairs,"

Dix recorded, "a strange, unnatural noise proceeded from beneath our feet. The door to a closet beneath the staircase was opened, revealing a female wasted to a skeleton."

At Medford, at Barnstable, at Groton—at every stop, the story was much the same. The mentally ill were "confined in cages, closets, cellars, stalls, pens." Inmates were "chained, naked, beaten with rods, and lashed into obedience." At Dedham, at Granville, at Plymouth—everywhere she went, Dix reported, "filth, neglect, and misery reigned."

Near Danvers, Dix wrote, she found "a condition of neglect and misery blotting out the faintest idea of comfort and outraging every sense of decency." In her journal, Dix described the fate of one young woman whose situation was typical of the way the mentally ill were treated:

> *There she stood, clinging to or beating upon the bars of her caged apartment, the size of which afforded space only for accumulation of filth—a foul spectacle. There she stood, with naked arms and dishevelled hair, the unwashed frame with fragments of unclean garments; the air so offensive that it was not possible to remain beyond a few moments without retreating for recovery to the outward air. To my exclamation of horror, the mistress replied, "We can do nothing with her."*

At Newton, Dix found an old man, ragged and dirty, chained to the side of a shed. His feet were mere stumps. Dix asked for the old man's story. She wrote down in her journal this shameful record:

> *The old man had been mentally ill for twenty years. Until the town had established the poor farm a few years before, this man, along with other paupers, sick and infirm, had been annually auctioned off to the lowest bidder. Each year this poor wretch had had a new master. For the major part of twenty years he had been chained in sheds and outhouses about the community.*
>
> *One winter when he was being kept in an outhouse, his keepers being warmed and clothed, did not "reckon how cold he was" and his feet froze. Since then he had not been able to walk. I asked why he was kept in chains. The reply was, "Oh, he can crawl, and when he gets mad, he might do some damage."*

Dix's travels forced her to endure her own sorts of punishments. She trekked through streets in rain, snow, and sleet. She rode in jouncing carriages and uncomfortable trains. She snatched an hour of sleep in unheated taverns and waited in deserted inns for the next coach. But Dix was never idle. She read articles on new treatments for the mentally ill. She kept her Bible close at hand.

In small ways, Dix tried to lessen the pain and suffering that she witnessed daily. She often brought gifts for the mentally ill, such as clothing, books, or magazines. She lingered at times to talk with a lonely inmate or simply to hold a patient's hand.

Her efforts did not go unappreciated. One grateful inmate wrote to thank Dix for her thoughtful gift, referring to her arrival as a "heavenly visit."

Dorothea Dix kept at her task until, in December 1842, the months of traveling were finally over. Dix came home to Boston. She was saddened to hear of the death of Rev. Channing, her friend and guide.

Mrs. Channing told Dix that just before he died, Channing whispered, "Tell Dorothea to persevere."

Dix quietly replied, "I shall never cease to mourn his loss."

But there was little time for Dix to grieve. Within a month, she had to have her report ready for the state legislature. She got to work immediately, reviewing and reorganizing her notes. She spent her days and nights writing an account of her travels that would force the people of Boston to take notice.

In just a few weeks, she had written a 30-page document. She called the report a "memorial" of her observations. It was a vivid record of her journey, a record of deprivation and cruelty. Perhaps most of all, it was a portrait of people who had been cast aside by family and community.

"I tell what I have seen," she began, "painful and shocking as the details often are." She continued:

> *I come to present the strong claim of suffering humanity. I place before the legislature of Massachusetts the condition of the miserable, the desolate, the outcast. I come as the advocate of the helpless, forgotten, and insane; of beings sunk to a condition from which the most unconcerned would start with real horror.*
>
> *If my pictures are displeasing, coarse, and severe, my subjects, it must be recollected, offer no tranquil or refined features. The condition of human beings, when reduced to degradation and misery, cannot be exhibited in softened language or adorn a polished page.*

The memorial presented the evidence of mistreatment that Dix had collected. There was the woman at Danvers. There was the man at Newton. There were hundreds of similar cases—too many, in fact, for Dix to describe in detail. Dix ended her memorial with a call to action. She put her "sacred cause" in the hands of the state's lawmakers:

> *Your action upon this subject will affect the present and future condition of hundreds and thousands. In this legislation, as in all things, may you exercise that wisdom which is the breath of the power of God.*

Before the memorial was printed and distributed, Dix gave a copy to Samuel Howe, now a member of the state legislature. Howe had agreed to present her report to his fellow lawmakers.

Howe, Sumner, and other leaders had supported Dix's survey. Now, Dix had provided them with the evidence they needed to make the case for more, and larger, mental hospitals. Howe urged the legislature to endorse the report and to increase funds to relieve the plight of the mentally ill.

"I presented your memorial this morning," Howe wrote to Dix in January 1843. Howe knew that it was Dix who deserved the credit for calling attention to this problem. "When I look back upon the time when you stood hesitating and doubting upon the brink of the enterprise you have so bravely accomplished," he wrote, "I cannot but be impressed with the lesson of courage and hope which you have taught even to the strongest men."

However, not everyone was impressed with Dix's memorial. Although reformers like Howe supported Dix, many officials across Massachusetts denounced the report as false and misleading. They sent angry letters to local newspapers, denying that mentally ill inmates were mistreated.

The debate went on for weeks. Dix again had the support of Charles Sumner, who visited some of the poorhouses and prisons that she described. Sumner saw for himself the men and women Dix's report so graphically depicted.

Sumner reported that "even the vivid picture" of Dix's report "does not convey an adequate idea of the unfortunate sufferers." Dr. Luther Bell, of the McLean Hospital, and other physicians cited similar cases that they had seen over the years.

On February 25, 1843, the legislature gathered to vote on a bill to improve conditions for the mentally ill. Dorothea was staying with Mrs. Channing at her Boston home while the lawmakers voted.

Dix waited for some word of the outcome in the Channings' library. A knock on the door announced that Howe had arrived.

"Miss Dix, your bill has passed," he reported.

The legislature had confirmed what Dorothea Dix knew was the case: health care for the mentally ill was inadequate throughout the state. The legislators voted to increase funding for the state's public hospitals, the only refuge for those who could not afford to pay for other treatment.

The vote was a victory for reform and a personal triumph for Dorothea Dix. Even more important, it was the first sign of a new era of medical care for the mentally ill.

6

Victory and Defeat

Dorothea Dix scarcely had time to enjoy victory before she began to receive requests from concerned people in other states, asking her to help them undertake similar reforms.

Maryland, Delaware, North Carolina, New York, New Jersey, Virginia, Pennsylvania—Dix would visit each of these states on more than one occasion. Her travels would take her to Indiana, Kentucky, Texas, Ohio, and the western territories. Between 1843 and 1845, she traveled more than 10,000 miles and visited hundreds of hospitals, prisons, and poorhouses.

One request for help came from the neighboring state of Rhode Island. Here, as in many other places, it was a common practice to auction off mentally ill people to serve as laborers on local farms.

Town governments paid farmers as little as a dollar a day to provide these people with decent food, clothing, and shelter. And, often, farmers accepted the money without making any effort to provide for their mentally ill laborers.

On April 10, 1844, an article by Dix appeared in the *Providence Journal* about one such case. In a small town called Little Compton, a man named Abraham Simmons had been "hired out" as a farm laborer. The farmer's wife showed Dix where Simmons was kept. His "home" was an unheated stone cell, barely big enough for him to stand. A solid iron door prevented his escape. The place was filthy and damp.

Simmons was "motionless and silent" when Dix approached him. She wrote that "his tangled hair fell about his shoulders; his bare feet pressed the filthy, wet floor." Dix recorded how she moved closer to him and then "struck against something which returned a sharp metallic sound. It was a length of ox-chain. The chain was connected to an iron ring which encircled a leg of the insane man."

"My husband," said the farmer's wife, "in winter rakes out half a bushel of frost, and yet he [Simmons] never freezes. Sometimes, he screams dreadfully; that is the reason we have the double wall and two doors in place of one. His cries disturbed us in the house."

"How long has he been here?" Dorothea asked.

"Oh, about three years. He was kept a long while in a cage first. But once he broke his chains and escaped. So we had this built, where he can't get out."

In response to such cases, Dix tried to enlist the help of wealthy people willing to contribute money toward an asylum. She decided to begin with Cyrus Butler, a businessman who was rich enough to help but hardly known for his generosity. Her friends in Rhode Island gave Dix little reason to hope that she might open the closed doors of this old man's heart. But she was not deterred and decided to pay a visit, unannounced, to the uncharitable Mr. Butler.

"What do you want?" he asked.

"If I am not intruding," she replied, "I wish to make a statement that will give the opportunity of a monument to your name as a benefactor to the poor that will never be forgotten."

"What do you want me to do?"

Dix explained the purpose of her unusual visit. She described the conditions at Little Compton. "Sir," she said to Butler, "I want you to give $50,000 toward the enlargement of the insane hospital in the city, to be called Butler Asylum."

It was not the kind of request that Cyrus Butler was used to. He agreed to donate $40,000, provided that an equal amount was raised from other sources. Dix urged the Rhode Island lawmakers to allot the money. A fund for the asylum was established, and it soon had more than enough contributions to satisfy Butler's terms. It was a second great success for Dix.

But it came too late for Abraham Simmons, who died before he could be moved to a more humane facility.

Dorothea Dix was now hailed as "the marvel of Rhode Island." And success followed success in quick order. In January of 1844, Dix presented a memorial, similar to her Massachusetts survey, to the New York state legislature.

"There is but one remedy," she told lawmakers there. "Provide hospitals and asylums where vigilant inspection and faithful care shall protect those who, in losing their reason, can no longer protect themselves." Although Dix did not receive approval for any new asylums, the New York legislature did agree to offer more funding for treatment at the state hospital.

In New Jersey, the state had made no provisions for the mentally ill. Here, too, Dix visited every jail, every poorhouse. She pleaded with the New Jersey legislators on behalf of those who were, she said, not capable of pleading their own cause.

In New Jersey, as elsewhere, Dix argued that it was the state's responsibility to protect and care for the disabled. Wherever Dix went, she advanced this new idea of public concern and commitment.

Her procedure in New Jersey was typical of her efforts. After a thorough investigation of the state's facilities for its mentally ill population, Dix conducted a newspaper campaign to make the public aware of the situation. She wrote articles that clearly described the terrible conditions facing the mentally ill. In this way, Dix tried to arouse public outrage and thus put pressure on the state's lawmakers. Finally, she issued a memorial to the legislature.

But however strong her case, Dix's work was not finished until she had convinced enough lawmakers to spend money on facilities or treatment programs. Their good words and intentions were not enough. Quietly but persistently, Dorothea Dix persuaded the states' political leaders to vote for new asylums, for enlarged hospitals, for more doctors. She was quickly becoming a skillful politician herself.

One of Dix's letters gives a good indication of just how convincing she could be:

> *The last evening, a rough country member who had announced in the House that the "wants of the insane in New Jersey were all humbug," after listening an hour and a half with wonderful patience to my details and principles of treatment, thus delivered himself: "Ma'am, I bid you good-night! I do not want, for my part, to hear anything more; the others can stay if they want to. I am convinced. You've conquered me out and out. I shall vote for the hospital. If you'll come to the House and talk there as you've done here, no man that isn't a brute can withstand you. And so when a man's convinced, that's enough."*

Many other tough politicians were convinced by the equally tough Dorothea Dix. "I encounter nothing," she wrote, "which a determined will does not enable me to vanquish."

On March 25, 1845, Dix received word that the New Jersey state legislature had voted to approve the construction of the New Jersey Lunatic Asylum.

It was, Dix said, her "first-born child."

Over the course of the next 35 years, Dorothea Dix would bring many "children" into the world. She had a direct hand in the creation of 32 state hospitals for the mentally ill. Nearly a hundred other asylums and institutions owed their existence to the attention she brought to a problem that had been hidden away in prisons and poorhouses.

For three months in 1848, Dix toured the jails and poorhouses of North Carolina, a state without public hospitals of any kind. "They say nothing can be done here," Dix wrote. "I reply, I know no such word." For weeks after her memorial was presented to the state legislature, Dix argued the case for a state hospital for the insane. She persuaded key legislators to support her request. On December 23, when the bill came to a vote, the hospital funding measure passed 91 to 10.

Dix was asked to help select a site for the new hospital. She found a lovely hillside southwest of the town of Raleigh. Topped by a grove of oak trees, the spot "overlooked a wide and peaceful valley."

"You will let us call it Dix Hill?" she was asked. Dix was too modest to agree to such a request. But her friends pressed her to accept some public honor for her efforts.

"If not in your honor, is there not someone dear to you whose memory you would like to perpetuate in this fashion?" Dorothea Dix did not have to think long about this. She asked to have the hospital named after her grandfather, Elijah Dix. And so the North Carolina hospital bore the name Dix Hill after all.

As she traveled about the country, Dorothea Dix became an honored and much-beloved figure. Known as a friend of the poor and outcast, she was equally welcomed in the wretched quarters that housed the insane and in the mansions of the rich and powerful. Dorothea Dix counted both the lowliest and the most distinguished people as her friends, including three presidents of the United States.

Whenever possible, she continued to bring gifts to ease the burden of the poor men and women she visited. In return, she often found herself the recipient of other people's generosity.

Mail companies forwarded her packages without charge. Railroad companies and stagecoach managers gave her free passes. When the head of a steamship company refused to take any money for her passage, he remarked, "The nation, madam, owes you a debt of gratitude it can never repay."

Her journeys took Dix from Maine to Mississippi, from Virginia to Wisconsin. By 1848, she had traveled more than 60,000 miles; she had visited more than 400 cities, towns and villages; she had directly observed more than 9,000 mentally ill people. This travel was often very difficult.

In North Carolina, for instance, she crossed the turbulent water of flooded streams and endured the delays caused by stagecoaches that broke down crossing the rough terrain. Dix learned to carry with her a little "emergency" bag of carpentry tools, nails, rope, and a can of axle grease.

Traveling up and down the Mississippi River on steamboats posed other kinds of danger. Sickness of many types often struck the passengers. On one trip, Dix noted, "We have on our boat both cholera and malignant scarlet fever." She began to come aboard with a supply of bandages, a basket of fresh fruit, and home remedies to help those who became ill.

Dix herself suffered from bouts of malaria. "Up again from malarial fever, off to Jackson, Mississippi, tonight," she wrote after one episode.

Throughout her travels, Dix was supported by a deep sense that her work was guided and blessed by God. To her friend Anne Heath, she wrote, "Heaven has greatly blessed my labors. I feel truly more and more that a leading Providence defines my path in the dark valleys of the world." To her English friends, she

wrote, "My success and influence are evidence to my mind that I am called by Providence to the vocation to which life, talents, and fortune have been surrendered these many years."

The range of Dix's interests broadened with her travels. She fought to reform the nation's prisons, to provide for poor soldiers and sailors, and to care for disabled children. And soon she prepared to fight a new battle. In 1848, Dorothea Dix developed a unique plan for helping the insane. She knew that the federal government had been giving away thousands of acres of publicly owned land for building projects such as roads, schools, and canals. But the United States still owned more than a hundred million acres of land.

Dix decided to ask the U.S. Congress to set aside a portion of government land for the benefit of the mentally ill. The land could be sold, but the money from any sale would go to the various states to build more asylums. In this way, Dorothea Dix would leave a permanent legacy for the people who most needed her help.

Dix appealed to Congress to set aside millions of acres for this purpose. She wrote a report to Congress that brought together her findings from every region of the country. At most, her report noted, there was only enough hospital space for one out of every five people who needed attention. The rest were "bound with galling chains, bowed beneath fetters and heavy iron balls." And with the increasing population of the United States, Dix noted, the number of mentally ill men and women was growing.

On June 27, 1848, her report was presented to the U.S. Congress. "I ask relief for the East, and for the West, and for the North, and for the South," wrote Dix. "I ask for the people that which is already the property of the people."

Dorothea Dix took up residence in Washington, D.C., and sought out political leaders to support her cause. She succeeded in gathering many supporters, but her efforts at securing legislation were repeatedly frustrated. Congress delayed action on her proposal. It was not until 1854, after six years of effort, that both the Senate and the House of Representatives at last approved the measure.

But no sooner was success at hand than the news came that President Franklin Pierce intended to veto the bill. The president said that Dix's proposal would oblige the federal government to provide for all kinds of poor people. Such charity, Pierce argued, was the responsibility of the states.

There was not enough support in the Congress to override the president's veto. Dorothea Dix's land bill was defeated.

7

"God Give Us Peace"

The defeat of the bill was a great disappointment to Dorothea Dix. Tired and discouraged, she returned to England, to the home of her dear friends, the Rathbones. There, she said, she would "take things easier."

But Dix was a person almost incapable of resting or forgetting the cause she had discovered so many years before. "It is true I came here for pleasure," she said, "but that is no reason why I should close my eyes to the condition of these, the most helpless of all God's creatures."

She began a tour of Europe's hospitals and treatment facilities for the mentally ill. "Look on a map," Dix wrote to Anne Heath. "You may trace my route." She traveled to 14 countries, including France, Italy, Turkey, Hungary, Austria, and Russia. She went to dozens of cities, from Paris to Moscow, from Rome to Trieste. And she visited hundreds of institutions for the insane.

In August of 1856, after two years abroad, Dix boarded a ship for the return voyage to New York. At age 54, she felt renewed, ready to resume her work.

"I have been brought home safely for some good purpose," she wrote upon her return. Certainly, there was plenty of work for her to do. She found hundreds of letters from people asking for her help. A hospital administrator needed more funds. The director of an asylum needed help to settle a staff dispute. A legislator wanted her advice and aid.

Dix went to work responding to these appeals for help. Between 1856 and 1861, she traveled almost continuously, crisscrossing the country. "I have traveled, out of ninety-three days and nights past, thirty-two days and nights," she observed. "I lie down now and sleep any hour I can, to make up for lost time."

"I am thankful I have come because I find much to do," she wrote from Texas, "and people take me by the hand as a beloved friend. My eyes fill with tears at the hourly heart-warm welcome, proving that I do in very truth dwell in the hearts of my countrymen."

At age 59, Dorothea Dix knew her country better than most people. She had seen so much of America on her travels. A life devoted to the mentally ill had been a life of service to her nation and its people.

She had spent the last 20 years working to change the way people thought about the mentally ill. Now, she wrote, a different kind of insanity was casting its shadow on the country. Wherever she traveled, Dix heard talk of war between the states. It was, she said, "downright madness."

As the Civil War approached, she wrote to Anne, "I thank God, dear Annie, I have such full uses for my time now, for the state of our beloved country, otherwise, would crush my heart and life."

Dorothea Dix was resting at the home of friends in Trenton, New Jersey, in April of 1861, when word came that the first shots of the Civil War had been fired. She left at once on a train headed south, first to Baltimore, Maryland, then to Washington, D.C. There, she volunteered her services to care for the wounded soldiers and to select nurses for the Union army. She asked no salary for her labors. She simply said that this was her duty.

Within weeks, Dorothea Dix was made Superintendent of United States Army Nurses, the first such title ever created and the highest post in the nation held by a woman. Her job was to train candidates for the Army Nursing Corps and to assign these nurses to military hospitals throughout the north.

But Dix's responsibilities quickly involved much more. She was called upon to organize huge amounts of medical supplies and food and to set up infirmaries in Washington, D.C.

Dix issued strict requirements for her nurses. "No woman under the age of 30 need apply to serve in the government hospitals," she insisted. "All nurses are required to be plain-looking women. Dresses must be brown or black, with no bow, no curls, no jewelry, and no hoop-skirts."

Such guidelines did not make Dix popular, but she wanted to avoid a rush of young, inexperienced girls looking for romance and adventure. She knew that there was neither romance nor adventure in war.

Dix didn't ask much about the past training of her nursing candidates. In fact, there were practically no trained nurses available. With the exception of a training program at the New York Infirmary, directed by Dr. Elizabeth Blackwell, there were no courses for nurses in the United States.

Blackwell, the first woman to become a certified doctor, helped Dix with the recruitment and training of nurses for the army. Several hospitals soon began to offer training programs for the war effort.

Within a few months, the horrors of war became apparent to Dorothea Dix and to those serving under her. Without adequate medical procedures, wounded soldiers on both sides of the war suffered greatly.

Many soldiers lay for days before their wounds were cleaned and bandaged. At makeshift hospitals, a steady stream of stretchers took the wounded inside while a processional of the dead were brought outside. The military hospitals were often crude places where disease and infection claimed many lives.

In the midst of suffering and death, Dix worked ceaselessly to see that military hospitals provided the best possible care. One report claims that during the four years of the war, she did not take a single day off from her work. A letter to Anne Heath confirms that Dix's days were "filled with crowding cares."

"I never had so few moments for myself," wrote Dorothea to her old friend.

Dix visited many military hospitals to inspect the work of her nursing corps and to observe the general operation of these hospitals. She noted inefficient or careless doctors. And Dix was quick to report such conditions to superior officers.

At a hospital near Washington, D.C., she arrived without introducing herself and began to inspect the wards. Soon, Dix was suggesting improvements and changes in the hospital's routine. At last, the doctor who was showing her around asked, "Madam, who are you that you presume to invade my domain and dictate to me, the officer in charge?"

She replied, "I am Dorothea L. Dix, Superintendent of Nurses, in the employ of the United States."

After she had left, the doctor in charge asked an associate more about this unusual visitor. "Why man alive," his friend replied, "don't you know her? She is as important as a major-general of volunteers, and if you have got her down on you, you might as well have all hell after you."

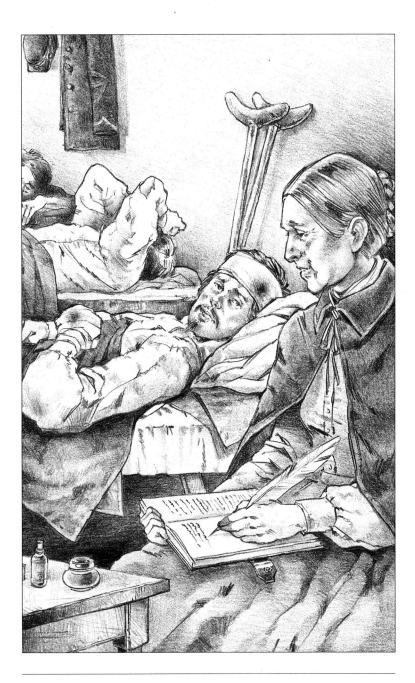

To many who worked with her, Dix seemed to be, as one nurse put it, "a stern woman of few words." But the war was deeply painful for her, and her stern face masked the emotions that she felt as she watched young boys suffer and die.

To Mrs. Rathbone, she wrote, "This war in my own country is breaking my heart." Always, as Dix left a hospital, she prayed, "God give us peace."

After the war's end, the U.S. Secretary of War, Edwin Stanton, asked Dix how she would like to have her services recognized. Should the Congress issue a special proclamation? A vote of money? "What would you like?" he asked.

She responded, "The flag of my country."

On January 25, 1867, Dorothea Dix received a box containing the flag of the United States, along with an official order that read:

> *In acknowledgment of the inestimable services rendered by Miss Dorothea L. Dix for the care, succor, and relief of the sick and wounded soldiers of the United States on the battlefield, in the camps, and hospitals during the recent war.*

In response, Dix replied, "No greater distinction could have been conferred upon me. No possession will be so prized while life remains to love and serve my country."

With the war over, Dix's friends hoped to see her again. So much time had been lost, and there were friendships to renew. But for Dix, too much time had been lost from the cause that was her life's work.

"I cannot come at present," she wrote to Anne Heath. "I am resuming care for the insane. I bid you farewell with a loving heart."

8

At Home

For 15 more years, Dix continued to devote her energy to the cause she had claimed as her own. Her asylums had come to be her "children," requiring her care and concern. She was always a welcome visitor. And she was always busy. "I have as much as I can do," she wrote Anne.

Anne Heath died in 1878. On her last visit to see her old friend, Dix noted that "life was fading for her into deep shadows."

For Dix, too, the light of life was fading. In 1881, Dorothea Dix returned to the state hospital at Trenton, the hospital that had been her "first-born child." She was worn out by her recent journeys. She stayed at the hospital for the rest of her life.

Dix wrote that she was "at home." She received many visitors and read letters from her friends. The Bible was always by her side.

On July 18, 1887, Dorothea Dix died. She was 85 years old. Dix was given a simple funeral. A passage from the Bible was read:

> *I was hungered and ye gave me meat. I was thirsty and ye gave me drink. I was a stranger and ye took me in, naked and ye clothed me. I was sick and ye visited me. I was in prison and ye came unto me.*

Her gravestone lies amid the peaceful, wooded knolls of Mount Auburn Cemetery, outside Boston. It bears the simple inscription: "Dorothea L. Dix."

Perhaps a more fitting epitaph would have been the words of one of her friends, Dr. Charles Nichols. He wrote:

> *Thus has died and been laid to rest, in the most quiet, unostentatious way, the most useful and distinguished woman America has produced.*

Dorothea Dix would be proud of the legacy she left on behalf of the mentally ill. When she entered the East Cambridge jail on that windy March day in 1841, there were only 14 asylums in the country, housing about 2,500 people. By the time of her death, there were 123 hospitals, caring for more than 50,000 mentally ill people.

Dorothea Dix had helped to establish 32 of these hospitals. She also worked to create the first federal hospital for the mentally ill, St. Elizabeth's, located in Washington, D.C. Through her efforts, more than half of the mentally ill population of the United States was receiving hospital care by the time of her death.

But Dix's legacy cannot be measured by hospital buildings alone. She made people aware of the cruelty that the mentally ill had to endure. She made people see this abuse and persuaded them to take action to stop it.

In the years after Dorothea Dix's death, the care of the mentally ill emerged as a significant branch of medicine. In 1909, the National Committee for Mental Hygiene was established. This group of doctors and psychiatrists promoted greater public understanding of mental illness. The committee stressed the need for more scientific and humane methods of treatment.

In the early 1900s, Sigmund Freud, an Austrian psychiatrist, proposed the idea that mental illness was related to conflicts that developed in early childhood. Freud's method of treatment, called psychoanalysis, was designed to help his patients to understand the causes of their illness.

Throughout the twentieth century, new theories about mental illness led to new ideas about treatment. The work of many doctors and scientists offered the mentally ill a better chance to recover.

But it was Dix who forced people to confront the humanity of the mentally ill, to recognize that these men and women deserved the same care and had the same rights as other sick people.

For thousands of years, the treatment of mentally ill people was a shameful and abusive chapter in the history of medical theory and practice. Dorothea Dix helped to bring an end to that tradition of neglect.

Dix brought more humane treatment, and hope, to the medically outcast. She dared to go places where no professional physician would go; she dared to care for those no one else cared about; and she dared to speak out.

Her voice—a strong and persuasive voice—was heard by people across the country and ushered in a new era of medical treatment for the mentally ill.

For Further Reading

Two full-length biographies of Dorothea Dix offer a complete picture of her life and work: *Dorothea Dix: Forgotten Samaritan*, by Helen E. Marshall (Russell & Russell, 1967), and *Stranger and Traveler*, by Dorothy Clarke Wilson (Little, Brown, 1975).

Many of Dix's memorials (surveys of facilities for the mentally ill) are found in *On Behalf of the Insane Poor* (Arno Press, 1971). This collection of state reports includes the Massachusetts memorial of 1843 as well as surveys for New York, New Jersey, Pennsylvania, Kentucky, Tennessee, Mississippi, North Carolina, and Maryland. Dix's national survey and proposal for a federal land-grant bill is also included.

Dix's views on prison reform have been published in *Remarks on Prisons and Prison Discipline in the United States* (Patterson Smith, 1967).

Nina Ridenour has written a history of mental illness in America: *Mental Health in the United States*, (Harvard University Press, 1961). Readers may also be interested in the first-hand account of mental illness by Clifford Beers, *A Mind That Found Itself* (Doubleday, Doran, 1929). First published in 1908, Beers's autobiography brought significant attention to the subject of mental illness.

An overview of mental illness can be found in *Diagnosing and Treating Mental Illness*, by Allan Lundy (Chelsea House, 1990).

Index